MAGNETIC Teaching

making God's Word stick in the lives of your teens

MAGNETIC Teaching

making God's Word stick in the lives of your teens

written and illustrated by Rick Bundschuh

Standard Publishing
Cincinnati, Ohio

Dedication

This book is dedicated to those young and old who have been the willing "guinea pigs" in my lifelong quest to present the everlasting precepts of God's Word with enough stickiness to assure it adheres to their heart and soul. Sorry about the continuing shock treatment, but you've gotta admit, it beats growing cobwebs in a pew.

All Scripture quotations, unless otherwise indicated, are taken from the HOLY BIBLE, NEW INTERNATIONAL VERSION®. NIV®. Copyright © 1973, 1978, 1984 by International Bible Society. Used by permission of Zondervan Publishing House. All rights reserved.

Edited by Leslie Durden and Dale Reeves
Cover and inside design by Dina Sorn
Cover photo by Dale Meyers

Library of Congress Cataloging-in-Publication Data:
Bundschuh, Rick, 1951-
    Magnetic teaching : making God's Word stick in the lives of your teens / written and illustrated by Rick Bundschuh.
      p.   cm.
    Includes indexes.
    ISBN 0-7847-0824-X
    1. Christian education of teenagers. 2. Teenagers--Religious life. I. Title.
BV1485.B83   1998
268'.433--dc21
                                                                                                     98-5818
                                                                                                                    CIP

© 1998 by Rick Bundschuh
All rights reserved
Printed in the United States of America

The Standard Publishing Company,
Cincinnati, Ohio.
A Division of Standex International Corporation.

05   04   03   02   01   00   99   98

5   4   3   2   1

Table of Contents

How to Use Magnetic Teaching Ideas 12

Stories That Stick

1. The Two Different Boys 15
2. Revenge 16
3. Professor Bonk 17
4. A Fair Trade 18
5. The Little Man of Nuremberg 19
6. And You Thought Nose Piercing Was Extreme! 20
7. I'm Gonna Sue! 21
8. Death under the Tree 22
9. It's in the Bag 24
10. For What It's Worth 26
11. Last Words 28
12. A Golden Thread 29

High-Impact Teaching

1. Lose It for Love 32
2. Words That Stick 34
3. Dying Man 35
4. Human Thank-You Card 36
5. Youth Group Time Capsule 37
6. The Stain of Sin 39
7. Dirt Magnet 40
8. New Kid in Town 41
9. Gone in a Flash 42
10. Defiling the Temple 43
11. Russian Roulette with God 45
12. A Personal Bible Version 46

Self-Adhesive Teaching

Creative Writing Ideas

1. Diary or Journal Entries 49
2. Paraphrase 50
3. Newspaper Creation 51
4. Letter Writing 52
5. Poems, Lyrics or Verses 53

Art Activities

6. Comic Strip 55
7. Clip-Art Collage 56
8. Buttons, Banners and Bumper Stickers .57
9. Family Crest 58
10. Ads and Billboards 59
11. CD Covers 60
12. Do-It-Yourself Booklets 61
13. Book Covers 63

Drama, Video and Theater

14. Pantomime 65
15. Paper-Bag Puppet Show 66
16. Interview and Talk Show 67
17. Bible Jeopardy 68
18. Captain Clay Video Show 69
19. Freeze Frame 70
20. Ask the Expert 71
21. Do It! 72
22. Biblical Post-It® Notes 73

Sticky Moments

1. Music Tasting Party 74
2. Taking God's Name in Vain 76
3. Instant Prayer Reminders 77
4. Filled or Flat? 78
5. Jerk Day 79
6. You Just Never Know 80
7. Do Not Open 81
8. Appreciation Party 82
9. The Cost of Freedom 83
10. Obituary Wake-Up Call 85
11. Honesty First 86
12. The Tapestry 88
13. How Am I Doing? 89
14. Bible, Be Gone 90
15. The Challenge of the Week 91

The Magnetic Field

1. Greenhouse 93
2. City Dump 94
3. Track and Field 95
4. The Cemetery 96
5. A Pigpen 97
6. A Wheat Field 98
7. A Pile of Manure 99
8. Polluted Water 101
9. A Bakery 102

Topical Index 105
Scripture Index 107

Introduction

"How was church this morning?" a friend asks. "Good," you say.

"What was the message about?"

"Er . . . um . . . ."

Most of what we hear evaporates quickly. And we hear and see plenty of information. There are more messages bombarding us today than ever before—more and more all the time.

Those who labor in the marketplace of ideas are aggressively working to make sure that their cat food, clothes, car and beverage pitches will lodge securely in our minds. That's why they invest millions of marketing dollars and hire the best and brightest talents available.

Along slogs Christianity.

Most of our meetings are low budget and low tech, directed by willing but lightly trained volunteers. We get an hour or two a week. The world gets the rest.

As Christians we too must wade into the marketplace of ideas. We do so knowing we offer the most valuable truth imaginable, a message that not only deserves to be heard and remembered but is the only one of eternal consequence.

Unfortunately, we who communicate this precious message have often unwittingly decided to use teaching methods that are among the worst ways to ensure that a message sticks to the souls of our learners. We get the message out, but few remember much of it.

Studies have shown that the more involvement and self-discovery a person has invested in a lesson, the longer they retain information. But we don't need studies to convince us of this. Common sense tells us the same thing. Remember studying far-off places in a geography class? Snooze! Remember how alive and vivid those same places became when you actually visited them?

Even though we know how people best grab and hold on to information, much of our teaching style in the Christian church continues to be one-dimensional, lecture-oriented and fizzless. The results are students who endure a lesson but absorb very little and teachers who are frustrated at the lack of impact that their teaching of the Word of God seems to be having in the lives of their students.

What are we to do? To compete on the budget-busting level of Madison Avenue or Hollywood is out of the question. Eloquent and gripping delivery is a gift that most of us don't have.

MAGNETIC TEACHING contains electrically-charged ideas that will fasten themselves to the minds of your students. Use them to increase the longevity of a given lesson or to add deep spiritual penetration to a particular program. These ideas will stimulate your teaching style and spark more ideas of your own. The stories, illustrations, object lessons, stunts and on-site activities presented here are sure to attract your students to God's Word. Each idea features suggested Scriptures and applications.

Not all ideas may seem workable for your particular group or situation. Some may be more fitting for a Sunday morning study and others for a midweek meeting. That's OK. Just choose and redesign to your liking. The plan is to put more hooks into your students than ever before.

We may not walk into the classroom with the budget of Madison Avenue or the bells and whistles of an MTV production but we do walk into the classroom with a much more exciting resource: the imagination of the Maker.

Allowing God's creativeness to run wild in our thinking will help us beat the world at its game. The message of the Kingdom will not only be heard, absorbed and bonded on the minds of our students, but it will kick out a lot of those competing messages placed there by the marketers of nonsense and lies.

That's why this book was written.

Rick Bundschuh
Kauai, Hawaii

How to Use Magnetic Teaching Ideas

Use This Book to Change Your Thinking

This is not merely a book of ideas to steal. It is also a philosophy, a way of thinking and acting when it comes to teaching about our faith.

To grab and implement the ideas without seeing the driving concept behind them is to get only part of the picture. The ideas in this book will soon run out, but a person who is committed to magnetic teaching won't go back to methods that don't stick.

Use This Book to Get Your Idea Juices Brewing

Not everything in this book will work for you or match your personality. Some things can be adjusted and tinkered with to better fit the needs of your particular students. Some ideas may simply spark totally new ones. Good!

Use This Book to Give Your Bible Study Sticking Power

As you thumb through the ideas presented, you may find something that zeros in on a lesson you already plan to teach. Or the ideas presented may suggest a subject to teach about. Either way, weave the magnetic teaching idea right into your lesson.

Use the Stuff in This Book in Various Ways

Mix up your teaching style. Do a story or illustration one week, go outdoors the next, followed by a self-adhesive activity on the third. Even magnetic teaching ideas can wear thin if the same teaching method is used too much. Variety makes the teaching stick better.

Section 1

Stories That Stick

Brief Tales and Illustrations

Jesus often taught volumes in mere moments. Filling an entire Sunday school hour with a lesson is not always the best bet. Now and then a lesson may be thrust in so thoroughly in a short matter of time that there is no need to continue. (Simply stop and do something else. Just because we have a time allotted to us does not mean that we must fill it with the noise of our own teaching. Remember, the hour was made for the kids, not the kids for the hour.)

People like and remember stories. A well-told story paints a mental picture. The hearers see the characters and imagine the surroundings, creating a movie in their mind. In so doing, they actually simulate dual sensory learning: hearing with their ears and "seeing" with their minds.

Stories were Jesus' primary teaching method. He understood the elements and staying power of a good story. His stories were simple, sometimes humorous, always profound. People loved to hear them.

Observe a good storyteller and audience in action and you will notice that the body language of the listener changes. Fidgeting stops, coughs are repressed and during any dramatic pause the listener often tilts in the direction of the storyteller. Storytelling draws people in.

Telling a Story

A good story needs to be "set up" properly with discussion or introduction. It can conclude with an explanation or moral, but it may sometimes be just as appropriate (especially with older listeners) to simply tell the story or parable and then say "go figure," allowing the hearer to wrestle with the application and meaning. This, by the way, was the device most often used by Jesus. His disciples had to beg for the explanations to his stories.

About the Stories

Many of the following stories are true. Some (such as the boy in the room of manure) are obviously tall tales. A number of these stories came from news service bureaus; others have circulated among storytellers for years. (A "story file" is helpful for any teacher.)

You can probably think of other Scriptures and applications that would work with these stories besides those suggested. Use them any way you see fit!

Stories That Stick

The Two Different Boys

Theme: Look for the good in every situation.
Scriptures: 1 Thessalonians 1:6; 5:16; 2 Corinthians 4:17, 18

Once there was a couple who had twin sons as different as night and day. One complained and found fault in everything. The other was a beaming optimist unfazed by any bad turn of events.

The parents hoped to bring their sons, particularly their dour one, to a more balanced outlook. They tried everything they could think of, but nothing changed the attitude of either child.

Finally, they came up with a desperate plan. They emptied two rooms. In the first they put every conceivable fun device that a child could imagine: video games, computers, trains and racetracks. The other room they filled with three feet of horse manure.

The parents then put the complaining, pessimistic son in the game-filled room and the sunny, optimistic son in the room filled with dung.

Several hours later they checked the progress of their experiment. In the game-filled room they found their first son huddled in a corner, weeping. The games had not even been touched.

"I thought that if I played with them I might break something," whined the boy.

When the parents opened the door to the second room, their other son was nowhere to be seen. Frantically the parents called for him. Suddenly he popped up from underneath a large pile of horse manure in the corner of the room.

"What are you doing under there?" his astonished parents asked.

"Well," said the boy with a bright expression, "I figure with so much manure, there's just got to be a pony in here somewhere!"

15

Magnetic Teaching

REVENGE

A True Story

Theme: Set aside anger and bitterness. While the husband's revenge has its ironic humor, this story is a good launching point for discussing how to handle our feelings of anger against someone who bugs us or wrongs us.
Scriptures: Proverbs 20:22; Matthew 5:38-42; Romans 12:17; 1 Thessalonians 5:15; 2 Thessalonians 1:6

For forty years Mrs. Anita Cemenescu waged war against her husband Marin's cigarette habit. She nagged, complained, scolded, berated and harangued him. Whatever her motivation, her efforts only stiffened his resolve to continue his habit in secret.

For forty years Marin Cemenescu hid his forbidden tobacco and sneaked off in corners like a schoolboy, fuming to himself that one day he would have his revenge.

At the age of 76, Marin died. But he had plotted his revenge well. When the will was finally read, it stipulated that in order to inherit his estate, Anita would have to take up the habit she so despised. The 63-year-old woman would be required to smoke five cigarettes a day for the rest of her life.

16

Stories That Stick

Professor Bonk

Theme: Be honest. God will reveal everything we would like to keep secret.
Scriptures: Proverbs 24:26; Colossians 3:9, 10; Titus 2:7

One year at Duke University, there were two guys in the chemistry class who did pretty well on all of the quizzes, labs and midterms. Going into the final, they were confident that they had top grades.

They were so confident, they decided to go to another college and party with friends over the weekend even though the chemistry final was on Monday. Things got out of hand at the party, and the two friends overslept. By the time they got back, they had missed the final.

The young men approached their chemistry teacher, Professor Bonk, and explained to him why they had missed the final. They told him that they had gone to another university over the weekend, and had planned to come back in time to study and take the test, but they had had a flat tire on the way back. They didn't have a spare and couldn't get help for a long time. So they ended up getting back too late to take the final.

Professor Bonk agreed that the two could make up the final the next day. Elated and relieved, they studied hard that night and went in the next morning at the time appointed.

The professor placed them in separate rooms and handed each of them a test booklet. Each one looked at the first problem, which was something about chemical solutions, worth five points. "Cool," they thought, "this is going to be easy."

However, when they turned the page for the next problem, they were unprepared for what they saw. It said: Which tire? (95 points)

17

Magnetic Teaching

A Fair Trade

Theme: Draw near to God, who wants to draw near to you. The idea of a humble trade-off between a great man and a child illustrates how God sees each of us as significant and wants to spend time with us.

Scriptures: James 4:8; 2 Corinthians 5:20, 21

After Albert Einstein, the famous and brilliant physicist, had been at Princeton for some months, local newshounds discovered that a twelve-year-old girl stopped by the Einstein home almost every afternoon. The girl's mother hadn't thought to ask Einstein about the ritual until the newspapers reported it. When she finally had the opportunity, she asked, "What could my daughter and you, the great Albert Einstein, have in common that you spend so much time together?"

Einstein replied simply, "She brings me cookies and I do her arithmetic homework."

Stories That Stick

The Little Man of Nuremberg

Theme: Rather than magnifying your shortcomings, maximize your God-given abilities. We complain about our lot in life: Our hair is too straight or too curly. We can't achieve the glamour or athletic prowess of others. This story shows what a person can do in spite of tremendous handicaps.

Scriptures: Matthew 25:14-29; Romans 8:28

The children ran down the street squealing in excitement, "The Little Man is coming! The Little Man is coming!" People left their shops and homes and quickly moved to a brightly bannered stage in the town center. A celebrity was coming to this little Bavarian town. People had heard of the Little Man, but this would be the first time they would actually see him perform. Anticipation bristled in the air as the whole village gathered.

Thick crowds formed long before Matthew Birchinger appeared on the stage. Known as "The Little Man of Nuremberg," he thrilled his eighteenth-century German audiences with spectacular tricks using cups and balls that have never been explained to this day. Wildly popular, he was one of the most famous stage magicians of his day. In addition he was an expert calligrapher and played four musical instruments, including the bagpipes.

Not bad for a guy who had no hands or legs and was less than 29 inches tall.

19

Magnetic Teaching

And You Thought Nose Piercing Was Extreme!

Theme: For true beauty, look inside. We are obsessed with "looking good." The Bible warns against putting much stock in our outward appearance, particularly when it means ignoring the real person inside. This look at actual styles from the past shows the lengths people have gone to in order to look attractive—according to the fashion of their day.

Scriptures: 1 Peter 3:3, 4; Proverbs 11:22; 31:30

People throughout the ages have done some pretty wacky things in the name of beauty. Consider the following:

- Fashionable eighteenth-century English women sometimes had wigs four feet high. These incredible hairdos were dusted with flour and decorated with stuffed birds, replicas of gardens, plates of fruit or model ships. Sometimes the wigs were so elaborate and expensive they were worn for several months.

  To help glue them together, the wigs were matted with lard (grease made of animal fat). Insects and mice found this tasty. Wire rat-proof caps and special pillows to cover and hold these works of art together were sold as accessories.

  Wig mania died out in 1795—a hair powder tax made them too expensive.

- Women of Egypt 1,500 years before Christ removed every hair from their heads with specially designed golden tweezers, then used cloths to buff their bald heads to a brilliant sheen.

- A hundred years later it was the rage among wealthy women to put a large cone of perfumed grease on top of their heads—and keep it there all day. As the hot Egyptian day wore on, the grease would melt and slowly drip down their bodies, covering their skin with a glistening oil slick and saturating their clothes with fragrance.

Stories That Stick

I'm Gonna Sue!
A True Story

Theme: Guard against greed. Although it is present to some degree in everyone, this news story exposes greed, dishonesty and their consequences in glaring detail.
Scriptures: 1 Timothy 6:9, 10; Luke 12:13-21

It was a minor bus accident in East Orange, New Jersey: a small bus with 15 passengers had a negligible collision: there was the crunch of metal, swirl of dust and then quiet.

A video camera at the scene recorded that 17 people showed up at the accident site. Good Samaritans racing to the aid of those supposedly injured in the crash? Not exactly. Each of these 17 onlookers were in a hurry to get on board the bus before the police arrived at the scene of the accident. They all claimed to have been aboard the bus at the time the accident occurred and predictably, they all were "injured" and wanted financial compensation for their stress and trauma.

What they didn't know was that the accident was staged by the East Orange police department and the 15 original passengers were planted by the bus company. Nor did they know that the whole event was captured on video cameras hidden inside and outside the bus.

They were all arrested.

21

Magnetic Teaching

Death under the Tree
Adapted from *The Canterbury Tales*, by Geoffrey Chaucer

Theme: Our wrongdoings always catch up with us. This classic tale is a sterling example of how evil gets its ultimate payback. As these characters find out, you really do reap what you sow!

Scriptures: Galatians 6:7; Romans 8:6

In a dark tavern three rowdy young men drank themselves silly. Not the most exemplary men, these three had spent their days and nights gambling, dancing, gorging and drinking.

One morning, still in a drunken stupor, they heard the church bells ring. Another funeral. (The Plague was claiming quite a few folks in those days.) One of them asked the tavern owner who had died and found to his shock it was one of their drinking buddies.

That did it for the drunken trio! They flew into a rage. Death had gone too far this time. It had ravaged the region for too long and had taken one of their pals.

They drew their swords and rashly swore that they were going to find the wicked monster Death and slay him! "Death is dead," they chanted as they marched out of town.

As they strode up the road, they came upon a hunched-over old man hobbling along the roadside. Belligerently, they demanded of him where they might find Death. The surprised old man fumbled for words. The roughians grabbed him by the throat and threatened to kill him if he didn't answer them. He told them they could find Death under a certain tree in the forest and described how they could find it.

Roaring with delight, the carousers set out to find the tree the old man had described. After much searching they found it and discovered to their surprise eight bushels of gold stuffed into the hollow base of the trunk. With this much gold, they could enjoy their wicked lifestyle forever!

Forgetting their quest to find and kill Death, the young men now tried to figure out how to get all this gold home without being robbed themselves or being accused as robbers by the townsfolk.

They decided to wait until nightfall to drag the bullion back to their homes. In the meantime hunger struck. They drew lots to see which one would go back to town to fetch food and wine for the rest. The youngest was chosen and set off.

After he departed, the pair waiting by the tree discussed how much wealthier they would be if they didn't have to split the gold three ways. So they plotted to kill the young man when he returned.

Meanwhile, the young man also entertained greedy notions. He figured that if he could be free of his companions all of the gold would be his. So he purchased some poison and slipped a lethal dose into two of the three wine bottles.

No sooner did he arrive back at the tree than the other men pounced upon him and killed him. Then they sat down to enjoy the food and guzzle the drinks he had brought.

The old man had told them the truth: Death indeed was under that tree!

Magnetic Teaching

9 It's in the Bag

Theme: God's values are not our values. One of the greatest follies a Christian can commit is to try to hold on to things that have no eternal significance. In this man's case it was his wealth, but there are plenty of other examples of short-lived pursuits: popularity, athletic prowess, academic or business accomplishments all turn to dust. Things done through the Spirit last forever.
Scriptures: Matthew 13:44; 1 Corinthians 3:12, 13

Once there was a man who valued material possessions highly. Even though he was a Christian, he put his love of things over that of other people and God.

One day a routine doctor's visit turned up some very bad news. The man had a terminal disease and would be dead within a month.

For most people, this news would dramatically change their perspective on life. But for this man, the thought of leaving his possessions caused him the greatest grief.

Every night he would beg God to allow him to take his "stuff" with him when he died. God always refused, but finally after days and days of pleading, God told him he could take one bag with him.

Even in his hospital bed he kept one hand on that bag. Finally he died holding on to the bag. Then he found himself standing in front of the pearly gates of Heaven. There, as in so many cartoons, stood Saint Peter himself, welcoming the new residents. As the man stepped forward, lugging an overfilled bag, Peter stopped him.

"I'm sorry, brother," Peter said. "We allow no luggage in here." The man protested loudly and insisted that he had permission to bring one suitcase. Mumbling that this was completely against policy, Peter went off to check the records and came back scratching his head.

"This is a first for me," Peter said to the man. "No one has ever been allowed to bring anything in here before, but I've been told you have permission."

Just at that moment, the bag tipped and the latch popped open. Out poured bright gold coins.

Puzzled, Peter looked down at the gold, leaned forward and whispered, "Of all things, why would you want to bring paving stones with you?"

Magnetic Teaching

For What It's Worth

Theme: Beware the lure of money. The astonishing sums of money produced in this review can spark great discussions about wealth, generosity, stewardship and the quest for happiness that many see in a pot of gold. How would we live our lives if we had that much cash?

Scriptures: Isaiah 55:1, 2; 1 Timothy 6:10; Matthew 6:24

When this book was written, basketball star Michael Jordan signed a contract paying him over $300,000 a game. That's $10,000 a minute, assuming he averages 30 minutes a game.

- Assuming $40 million in endorsements, he'll be making $178,100 a day, working or not.
- If he sleeps 7 hours a night, he makes $52,000 every night.
- Going to see a movie will cost him 7 bucks, but he will make $18,550 while there.
- If he boils a 3-minute egg, he'll make $370 while it boils.
- If he wanted to save up for a new Acura NSX ($90,000), it would take him a whole 12 hours.
- If he went to play a round of golf, it would cost him around $200 but he would make $33,000 while playing that round.
- He'd make about $19.60 while watching the 100-meter dash in the Olympics but about $15,600 if he watched the Boston Marathon until the first runner crossed the finish line.
- In the time it takes for the average person to eat in Michael's trendy Chicago restaurant for the average cost of $20, Jordan will make $5,600.
- If you were given a tenth of a penny for every dollar he made, your salary would be $65,000 per year.
- In one year he will make twice as much as all of our past presidents for all of

their terms combined.

But consider this:

Jordan would have to save 100% of his income for 270 years to have a net worth equal to that of Bill Gates.

And:

The average working man in Tijuana, Mexico considers himself lucky to make $50 per week.

Magnetic Teaching

Last Words
A True Story

Theme: Redeem the time. In this dramatic story of a man who made his last minutes count is a challenge for all of us to share our faith with those around us. You just never know when it will be their last chance to hear.
Scripture: Matthew 28:16-20

When Andrew Meekens boarded an Ethiopian Airlines jet, he had no idea that among the passengers was a group of terrorists intending to hijack the plane. Nor could he have imagined that it would be his last day on earth.

Surprising the pilot and crew, the hijackers took over the plane, demanding to be flown on a new course. Just off the Comoros Islands, the plane ran out of fuel and the pilot announced that he would be attempting an emergency landing in the water.

Suddenly Andrew Meekens, normally a reserved man, rose to his feet. A deeply committed Christian, he served as an elder in the International Evangelical Church of Addis Ababa. According to witnesses, he presented the good news of Jesus Christ to his fellow passengers and then invited people to respond. Moments later the plane crash-landed in the ocean. Meekens perished as did the hijackers and numerous others. Neither his body nor that of the hijackers (whose identity is still unknown) were recovered.

A surviving flight attendant said that about 20 people accepted Christ, including a fellow flight attendant who did not survive the crash.

Stories That Stick

A Golden Thread
A True Story

Theme: God is good. We cannot fathom his plans, but every once in awhile we see how God takes tragedy and evil and fashions immense good from them. This story is an example of the thread of glory with which God weaves his will.

Scriptures: Proverbs 19:21; Romans 8:28

Sometimes we mortals glimpse how God takes tragedy and transforms it into his glory. In this true story the golden thread of God's design runs where we might never imagine it would.

On Sunday morning, December 7, 1941 the dawn quiet was interrupted by the roar of low-flying bombers and the sudden blinding explosion of metal, fuel and flesh. It was a surprise attack on the United States Pacific fleet led by young Japanese commander Mitsuo Fuchida.

The attack killed and injured thousands of unsuspecting sailors and soldiers, launched the American involvement in World War II and made Mitsuo Fuchida a hero in his homeland.

The war ran its course. As the tide began to turn against the Land of the Rising Sun, boatloads of Japanese prisoners were shipped to an American POW camp nestled near the borders of Utah and Colorado.

Local residents directed a great deal of bitterness and hatred toward these "yellow-skinned devils." But in one exceptional case, a young American girl volunteered to work among the prisoners. She spoke no Japanese but endeavored to make their lives more comfortable with tireless energy and kindness.

Eventually, her story became known to the inmates. She was Peggy Covall, college-aged daughter of an American

Magnetic Teaching

missionary couple who had been brutally slain—beheaded—by the Japanese army as they overran the Philippines. She had overcome her own grief and hatred to reach out in forgiveness to those who had butchered her parents. Her faith and love astonished and amazed the Japanese POWs who met her.

Meanwhile, the war was not going well for Mitsuo Fuchida. Most of his friends had been killed or wounded, his nation suffered defeat in battle after battle and the inevitable loss of the war loomed near.

Two atomic bombs took the remaining fight out of the Imperial Army. Mitsuo was crushed with the pain and humiliation of defeat and the sorrow of so much vain suffering and loss. The emptiness in his heart tortured him until a returning POW friend told him the strange story of Peggy, the loving Christian girl left parentless by Japanese invasion forces.

Fuchida became desperate to know the God of this amazing faith. His search came at an interesting time. Western missionaries were flooding into Japan, trying haltingly to explain the gospel in a way that made sense to the culture. They were largely unsuccessful . . . until Mitsuo came to faith in Christ.

His status as a national hero gave him instant credibility in Japan and his ease in understanding his own people made him an effective evangelist. He led thousands of his people to give their lives to the Savior.

The golden thread had run through the lives of the Covalls. Their calling to the mission field, their untimely death, their daughter's faithfulness, a POW's story, the heart of one of the war's most infamous men—all weaving through the lives of thousands. The thread runs still.

Section 2

High-Impact Teaching

Sometimes teaching does more than stick on a student—it embeds itself permanently. The ideas in this chapter are ones that have the potential never to be forgotten. Because of their novel and sometimes outrageous nature, you'll want to be selective about how you use them. They are not the kind that you will be able to repeat with the same group of kids.

As with other teaching ideas in this book, some are best used as part of a lesson or an illustration of a point and others will pretty much dominate the teaching time.

Evaluate your group to make sure that the ideas you select will go over. The chemistry of any group varies from year to year. Use your wisdom and instinct as you pick through these gutsy ideas which work because they are outrageous, hard-hitting or wild. Be very intentional when setting up these teaching times. Make sure to pick the right time, the right age group and the right moment to unleash one of these on your kids.

Magnetic Teaching

Lose It for Love

Theme: Sacrifice for others as if sacrificing for Jesus.
Scriptures: Matthew 25:35-40; Mark 9:41; Luke 3:11; Acts 11:29
Materials: A set of hair shears; stool; apron; floor covering; a person to act as a barber; clipboard with paper and pen; a few folks to help put up some bucks for missions.

For this lesson you need access to some funds that can be directed towards people in need. (Compassion International, World Vision and others have programs which help those suffering in Third World countries.)

At the front of the room, have your stool and barber ready to go. Begin by pointing out the horrendous plight of people in the world and Christ's teaching on our need to sacrifice in order to ease the pain of those who suffer.

Tell your students, **"I have at my disposal a considerable amount of money that could be used to relieve the suffering and hunger of many children living in poverty. I will give this money to you to send to the poor, but you must first earn it by making sacrifices. I am authorized to give $25 to Christian charitable organizations for every guy who will allow himself to get a buzz job from our butcher . . . er, barber here, and to every girl who will commit to going to school for one week without wearing any makeup."** (If these don't work for your group because you already have a makeup-less class of skinheads, simply create your own sacrifice. Going without TV or music for a week, being at a 5:00 A.M. prayer meeting for five days in a row and the like.)

Let kids decide if they are willing to pay such a small price for providing mercy for the suffering. You also may wish to give kids an option of kicking in their own $25 if they can't bring themselves to get a buzz cut or be without makeup but still want to sacrifice.

Every time a kid jumps up for a haircut or signs her name for a week as "plain Jane," count out 25 bucks. See who is really willing to sacrifice.

If a girl gets her head shaved, kick in $100.

Magnetic Teaching

Words That Stick

Theme: Words and labels we give others have an impact for good or bad.
Scriptures: Proverbs 12:18, 19; Matthew 12:34-37; James 3:5-10
Materials: Large peel-and-stick labels such as Avery® Labels; felt-tip pens

Give each student two sheets of labels and a felt-tip pen. Ask them to write on one sheet slurs, degrading names, insulting terms or labels that kids give to other kids. On the other sheet write down a list of names, terms or labels that are given to people who are liked and admired.

Ask for two volunteers to stand in front of the group. On one volunteer have your teens stick the negative labels, on the other the positive labels. Make each volunteer stand there as you read the various labels as if you are describing the teen they are stuck on.

Discuss how it feels to be labeled a loser, an outcast or jerk by others. You may not have to push too hard. Most kids will get the point that sticking a label on people by our words and actions can have good or bad results. Encourage your students to think of ways they can put affirming labels on others.

Good luck getting the labels off of your volunteers.

34

High-Impact Teaching

Dying Man

Theme: Facing death, we must reassess our values.
Scripture: 1 Corinthians 15:52-57
Materials: Index cards; pencils

From time to time a devout Christian is given the tough news that he or she has only a short time left on this earth. Reactions to the news vary. On occasion some of these folks are willing to come in front of a group of young people who have their whole lives in front of them and share deeply from their hearts. All you need to do is gently ask.

The insights that people have who are looking at a defined timetable are usually well worth considering. Ask your guest if questions would be permitted. Then, have your students write them on index cards. These discussions provide discovery moments that can never be duplicated. They can be very sobering and emotion-laden. Students who often are rowdy usually settle right in during this kind of sharing time.

Magnetic Teaching

Human Thank-You Card

Theme: Express gratitude.
Scriptures: Colossians 1:11, 12; 1 Thessalonians 5:18; Hebrews 3:13
Materials: Lots of felt-tip pens; individual willing to be the "card"; camera

The next time your youth group has an occasion to thank someone or is considering a lesson on thankfulness, try sending a thank-you card of a human variety.

In advance, ask a boy to come wearing his bathing suit under his clothes. At the appropriate time in the lesson, tell your students, **"Today we are going to say thank you in a very graphic way. We are going to create a human thank-you note."**

Have your students think of what they want to say to the person(s) that you are thanking while your "card" strips to his bathing suit. Hand out felt-tip pens and let them go to it! (Make sure the kind of markers you use are water-based and will come off your volunteer fairly easily.)

Dress up your thank-you card and send him off to "bare" the glad tidings of your group. (Take a few photos during the process.)

High-Impact Teaching

Youth Group Time Capsule

Theme: Consider God's direction and plans for your life.
Scriptures: Jeremiah 29:11-13; Psalm 40:5; Proverbs 19:21; John 14:16, 17
Materials: A solid, tightly sealed container that can be stored as a time capsule for ten years; a person willing to be accountable for the time capsule, who will contact those listed inside when it is time to be opened

This activity can impact both the present and the future. To make sure it works well, spend several weeks publicizing your time capsule event.

Ask your students to bring any objects that reflect the trends and thinking of the day as well as an evaluation of where they are in their spiritual lives.

Here are a few suggestions:
- Photographs of themselves. (You may want to have a Polaroid camera available to take up-to-the-minute pictures.)
- Samples or magazine pictures of current fads, popular music, clothes or anything else that your students think is cool.
- A written statement of what God has been doing in their lives and where they think they might be ten years from now.
- Personal mementos of things that were important to them with an explanation of why each item has memory or value.

Before you assemble the time capsule, discuss with your students how to understand God's direction and plan for their lives. Read the Scriptures listed above as well as Matthew 7:21; Mark 3:35; and Romans 12:2. Then involve your students in a discussion with

37

Magnetic Teaching

questions such as:
- **How does a person know what God's will and plan is?**
- **What decisions, habits and choices that we make now will help or hurt us ten years from now?**
- **What things that we spend a lot of time, money and effort on today will matter little in ten years and what things will still be worth while after ten years?**

Let your students know that every effort will be made to contact them in ten years for a time capsule opening party, with the announcement going to their current home addresses. (Make sure they put their parents' address in the box.)

High-Impact Teaching

The Stain of Sin

Theme: We are all sinners who need forgiveness.
Scriptures: Isaiah 1:18; Joel 2:12, 13; Romans 3:10-18; 4:8; 7:21-25
Materials: A large bottle of food coloring; a rag to dry students' hands; one pair of rubber gloves. (A restaurant supplier can sell you large bottles of food coloring for much less than a grocery store.)

We are born with a sinful nature in our flesh. We are born with the stain of sin on us that we cannot remove. The good news of the gospel is that Jesus Christ removed the penalty for our sin by his death on the cross.

Not only are we born with the stain of sin, but sometimes we can stain our lives permanently by wrong actions. While God forgives all our sins, the stains remain. He gives us a new nature to counter the old one but doesn't make the old nature instantly vanish. It must be put to death in a day-by-day battle.

To make this point in an "indelible" way, put undiluted food coloring in a container (blue works well and is tough to get out; but red could represent the crimson stain which God makes whiter than snow). Have each student dip at least one finger in the solution. (Make sure they dry their fingers before touching anything.)

After your students have all dipped their fingers in the food coloring, begin your discussion about the stain of sin.

Your kids will find that they will have a difficult time getting the food coloring off their hands. Let them know that the stained fingers can create a good opportunity to share their faith with others.

39

Magnetic Teaching

Dirt Magnet

Theme: Confess your sins daily.
Scripture: 1 John 1:9
Materials: A roll or two of clear 3-inch packing tape (you know, the super sticky stuff); scrap paper; pens; folding chairs; two good-natured volunteers

Wrap two volunteers with tape, sticky side out all the way up to their necks.

Give the rest of the group scrap paper and ask them to write words that might describe negative or wrong things that a person might think, say or do in the process of a day. Encourage everyone to write on as many scraps of paper as they wish.

Have your group sit in chairs in two parallel lines about four feet apart facing each other. Have one taped person start at one end of the chairs and the other taped person start at the opposite end. At your signal each taped person should try to make it through the gauntlet to the other end of the rows. While these players are going through the gauntlet, those seated on either side should try to stick as many pieces of paper on them as possible without leaving their seats. The winning "Dirt Magnet" is the one with the least pieces of paper stuck on.

Use this game as an illustration of how we collect scraps of sin that need to be confessed and cleaned every day.

40

High-Impact Teaching

New Kid in Town

Theme: Reach out in love to others, particularly newcomers.
Scriptures: James 2:1-4; Titus 1:8; 1 Peter 4:9
Materials: A kid that none of the other students know. This should be a "plant" who is prepared for his role in advance. (You probably can find a kid like this in the youth group of another church across town.)

Before the meeting, contact your teenage "plant" and explain what you are trying to do in this lesson, which is to test the group to see how they treat a new kid. During the meeting, the teen should take a shy and passive role, letting others initiate conversation. Have your teen note which kids (if any) come up to start a conversation or introduce themselves.

Run a typical meeting. Make the focus of your lesson reaching out to others. At some point, say something like this:

"Today we have the privilege of having a new student in our midst. Let's find out about the warmth and friendliness of our group today."

Introduce your secret plant and ask for honest answers to questions such as these:

- **Did anyone greet you when you came today?**
- **Did you feel the group moved toward you and welcomed you in?**
- **Did you feel accepted or that people were interested in you?**

Some may complain that they were "set up." The point is that we must be thinking of others at all times, particularly those who are new among us.

Magnetic Teaching

Gone in a Flash

Theme: God completely removes the sins of those who come to him.
Scriptures: Psalm 103:12; Isaiah 43:25; Hebrews 8:12
Materials: Flash paper (found in magic stores); felt pen; matches or lighter

For a quick way to demonstrate how instantaneously and absolutely God forgives and takes away our sin when we come to him, get your hands on some magician's flash paper. Have your students write various sins that are common to their age group. When you set a spark to it, the flash paper will go up in flames so quickly that it can be tossed in the air and will literally evaporate in an instant. It leaves no residue or ash.

You may want to experiment with this stuff before trying it out on the kids. Note: Don't tell them you are using flash paper. Let the suddenness of their sins' disappearance astonish them.

High-Impact Teaching

Defiling the Temple

Theme: We must use caution about what we allow into our minds and hearts.
Scriptures: 1 Corinthians 3:16, 17; Hebrews 3:1
Materials: A CD with really terrible lyrics; CD player; paper and pencils

This activity is a shocker. Check with your leadership team before attempting it.

Get your hands on some CDs with warning labels about vulgar and explicit language. (Where? Ask your kids. Most likely they have some of them at home.) Suck it up and listen to the CD. Pick the track with the foulest language on it.

Start a discussion on what it means to defile the temple of God, using the suggested Scriptures. Ask, **"Who is the temple of God? What does it mean to defile something? How would a person defile your room? How do people defile themselves?"**

Encourage your students to consider the fact that we have control over what enters our minds. We can let pollution in or keep it out.

Make no comment or judgment about the music that you are going to play—the impact of this lesson comes by allowing the teens to make the judgment call themselves. Tell your students, **"I came across this little recording that is very popular with many of your friends. I want to play it for you. You listen carefully to the words and then you decide if this fits the definition of defiling ourselves."**

Play the CD. Be prepared for a shocked look on the faces of some of your students (as if to say, "How could you play that in church?"). Be as stoic as possible.

When the cut is done, ask students a few prodding questions like these:

- **Would you consider this music to be defiling? Why or why not?**
- **Does it offend you that I would play**

43

Magnetic Teaching

this music in church? Why or why not?
- Would it offend you if one your friends played it when you were around?
- What would you do if your friends were really into this music and played it while you were hanging around them?
- What would you say if a friend complained to you about the content of a song you enjoyed?
- Is pornography verbal as well as visual?
- What might be Christ's comment about what we have just listened to?

Some students may argue with other kids. This stimulation is good. Act as an inquirer and stimulator of the learning and debate that is taking place.

44

High-Impact Teaching

Russian Roulette with God

Theme: Only a fool plays games with God and his soul.
Scriptures: Proverbs 1:7; Psalm 14:1; Matthew 7:26
Materials: A bunch of boiled eggs; one raw egg; several volunteers; towels

Like other wild but high-impact ideas in this book, be sure to get permission from your leaders to do this stunt.

As you discuss the nonchalant way with which many people approach their lives, particularly those who repeatedly snub God, note that this is very much like playing Russian roulette. Rather than using a gun to demonstrate this, you will be using eggs. The Bible clearly tells us that we reap what we sow. For those who sow to the flesh it is only a matter of when—not if—they will end up in destruction. Some of the foolish things kids do that you can mention are drugs, stealing, lying, sex, vandalism and so forth—things that teens think they might "get away with."

To illustrate some of these "foolish things," invite several volunteers to come up to the front, one at a time, and select an egg by pointing to it (don't let them touch it themselves). Make sure you cover the floor under them with a towel. Crack the egg they have picked over their head, calling it "drugs" or "stealing" or whatever. Each time you make a point, have a different volunteer come and take his chances with an egg. Discuss how people foolishly think they will get things right with God when they are older. This again is like playing Russian roulette with our lives. Continue cracking eggs over students' heads until the unlucky one gets messy.

Magnetic Teaching

A Personal Bible Version

Theme: Trust and obey God even when it conflicts with your desires.
Scriptures: Matthew 6:24; John 14:15
Materials: Worn-out or inexpensive Bible; sharp scissors or X-ACTO® knife

It's a nasty habit: we sometimes build our faith on our favorite Bible passages but ignore the rest. God does not allow us the option of redesigning his Word to fit our tastes. To clearly illustrate what it means to accept some Bible truths and forget others, use this shocker.

Thumb through a Bible as you discuss the fact that there are a number of difficult and even unpleasant teachings in the Bible. For example, read Matthew 18:21, 22 and say something like this: **"Most of us would agree that forgiveness is fine and good. But let's face it—this business about forgiving seventy times seven is extreme and can't be seriously recommended for anyone."** With that, whip out your scissors or X-ACTO® knife and slice that teaching right out of the Bible, crumple it up and toss it on the floor.

Continue deleting passages that are hard or distasteful. In fact, start ripping whole books and blocks of teaching right out of the Bible. Subjects to delete include anything about Hell, loving enemies, God killing people, weird stuff from Revelation and Old Testament visions of God.

In a few minutes you will have a custom-made Bible. All the offensive bits will have been removed. This easily demonstrates exactly what people do in their hearts who won't take God at his Word. Of course, you will then need to assure your students that the entire Bible is the Word of God and every part of it is true and trustworthy.

Section 3

Self-Adhesive Teaching

While stories, object lessons, stunts and on-site ideas work to increase the magnetic attraction of a lesson, the very best way is good old hands-on learning. The role of a teacher using self-adhesive methods is really that of a guide. The teacher keeps everyone on the trail, makes sure that no one is straggling in their understanding and sets the pace for the journey. The guide knows the landscape. She knows where the students need to travel as they explore a particular section of the Bible and ensures that everyone makes it to that destination. The guide encourages, controls and directs the discovery being made by the kids themselves.

Here are some tips:

- Most of these ideas are best done in groups of eight or fewer students. If you have a large number of teens, simply pare them down to workable groups and have an adult helper or resource person move among several of them to monitor their effort and give clarification.
- Always give clear and precise instructions. Write out the instructions for each group, if necessary.
- Be sure to have materials and work areas prepared in advance.
- It is important to allow students to share the results of their energy and creativity with the whole group. They can feel slighted if their work is not displayed.

Magnetic Teaching

- The length of each activity varies. Give your students clear time limits and remind them during the process of their work how much time they have left to finish.
- You can mix up various self-adhesive ideas so that each group is exploring the same passage of Scripture, but using a different method to do so. For example, suppose you are looking at the parable of the prodigal son. One group could be drawing a cartoon strip depicting that story while another works out a drama and a third writes the journal entries for various people in the story. Each group would then present its version of the parable or the application of the truths behind it.

SELF-ADHESIVE CREATIVE WRITING IDEAS

Diary or Journal Entries

Have students read a passage of Scripture and report back what they have read by imagining what might have been noted in the diary or journal of some of the people involved. (Note: Guys write journals; girls write diaries. It does make a difference in most groups.)

For example, if you are studying the anointing of young David, you might have each group select and write a journal entry from the vantage point of David, Samuel, David's brothers or David's father. This would give you at least four points of view for the same incident.

The use for reflection via a diary or journal entry is limitless. Youth can be prodded to reflect on what the journal entry might be of a girl who is new in school, a boy who is unpopular or lonely, two friends God uses in spite of themselves, a teenager who is confused about important choices and so forth. In other words, this idea is not limited to exploring the perspectives of biblical people only.

Magnetic Teaching

Paraphrase

A great way to see if your teens can make heads or tails of a Bible passage is to ask them to rewrite it in a simpler way. Perhaps they could write Romans 8:1 in such a way that a little kid would get the point. Or they could paraphrase a passage so a person from a primitive tribe or an unbeliever off the street would understand. A passage of Scripture that can be retold in a simpler manner is understood.

Here is what Romans 8:1 might sound like for a clueless person: "When you believe in Christ, you will be out of hot water with God."

Self-Adhesive Teaching

Newspaper Creation

Reporting events from your Bible lesson in the mode of a newspaper is not only loads of fun, it gives everybody something to do and can result in a great take-home piece when you are all done.

After you establish your biblical basis, have students read the passage and then, staying true to the facts of the text, create a newspaper of the day that covers those facts and ideas. You can have writers for front page news and headlines, food and entertainment, the sports page, etc. Artistic types can create cartoon photos of various situations or design ads or the comic page, amplifying the text in a clever way.

With a handy laptop computer, a simple publishing program and a copy machine, you can create an instant newspaper that could be completed, printed and distributed by the end of the meeting.

Imagine the fun you could have creating a newspaper (or several of them from different points of view: Christian, Jewish and Roman) of the events that took place in Acts 2!

Magnetic Teaching

Letter Writing

Writing imaginary letters between people in the Bible is a great way to help students understand a text they are studying. Doing a discipleship study? Imagine letters home from the disciples to their families struggling to understand why they would abandon homes, careers and friends to follow Jesus.

Letters can be a great way to close a meeting. Writing a letter to God, to someone else or to oneself can be a great way to summarize and apply a variety of truths. (Note: This would be one situation where it would probably be inappropriate to ask students to share with the group.)

Self-Adhesive Teaching

Poems, Lyrics or Verses

Have your students report their exploration of the Bible with poetry. Musically inclined teens may want to create their poetry as words to a song. For some serious silliness, use well-known advertising jingles or the tune to some corny song.

For older students, try haiku poetry, which is unrhymed verse with three lines having five, seven and then five syllables. Haiku is great for your rhyming-impaired students!

Magnetic Teaching

SELF-ADHESIVE ART ACTIVITIES

Creating art as a response to Bible truths is both fun and effective. Art activities tend to take time, so be sure to consider that when planning your schedule. Provide clear instructions and prepare materials in advance.

Some kids are natural artists and some struggle with stick figures. Encourage your students to think of themselves as the visionaries behind the art project rather than the fine artist who would do the final work. Sketches and stick figures are fine. The idea is to drive the lesson's point home. Proficiency doesn't matter.

Older teens will take to art projects as fast as younger ones if the activity has an obvious purpose. For example, creating a puppet show might not be the kind of thing that a sophisticated group of seniors would get into—unless they were creating a show to put on for the kindergarten class. In that case, they would throw themselves into their work.

Check out some of these activities and see if they might work for you.

Self-Adhesive Teaching

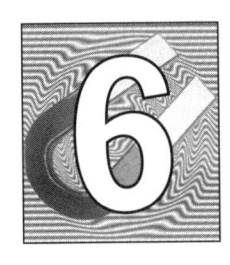

Comic Strip

Create a comic strip based on an idea, incident or event in the Bible. Have students work individually or in groups with each teen doing a panel of the story. A comic strip is a great way to get an overview of a person in Scripture.

For example, by breaking up incidents about Paul found in the book of Acts and assigning a different incident to each student or group of students, the life of the apostle could be tracked in a fascinating fashion.

Magnetic Teaching

Clip-Art Collage

By getting your hands on piles of old magazines, pages of clip art, blank paper, felt-tip pens and rubber cement, your students can express biblical truth in the form of a clip-art collage.

When doing collages, which can be in mural or comic-strip form, draw or paste in dialog balloons. You can create one large collage which stands alone or get several groups busy making a series which expresses different ideas or expands on a longer passage.

For example, create a collage to retell the story of the fool and his money or to highlight its application using modern examples. (See Luke 12:13-21.) Display the results for a few weeks. To help cement the lesson into your students' minds, quickly review the stories represented by the collage at every meeting.

Self-Adhesive Teaching

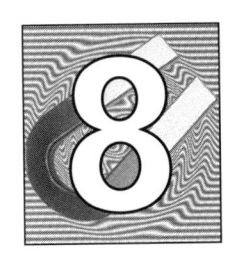

Buttons, Banners and Bumper Stickers

Using slogans and symbols, students can succinctly state the theme or idea of a biblical passage.

A typical assignment might sound something like this: **"Imagine that bumper stickers were put on the back of chariots, donkeys, carts and wagons during the ministry of John the Baptist. Read Matthew 3:1-17; 11:1-19; 14:1-12 and then come up with possible bumper stickers both for those who were involved with or supported John's ministry and for those who were skeptical."**

Bumper sticker paper (peel-and-stick labels) and button materials can be purchased at most office supply stores. Banners can be made from computer paper intended for that purpose or rolls of newsprint paper.

Magnetic Teaching

Family Crest

Family crests or coats of arms were a common thing centuries ago in Europe and Asia. Placed on a family's crest were all the elements that signified the virtues of that family.

Your students can have a load of fun and learn something too by creating a new version of a family crest or coat of arms as part of a Bible study. When studying a personality in Scripture, a coat of arms could be devised for that individual. For example, students could read the account of the struggle between Moses and Pharaoh. They might then create a coat of arms for Moses, Pharaoh and possibly even Aaron.

Application of biblical principles can be displayed by a coat of arms as well. What might the family crest of your youth group look like? What might be on the coat of arms of a person trying to live for Christ in high school?

Since much of the art on a family crest is symbolic, make sure that your students explain what each symbol stands for when they share their creations with the group.

Self-Adhesive Teaching

Ads and Billboards

Advertisers use ads to get their message across. God's message can be communicated the same way.

After reading a passage of Scripture, ask your students to create an ad campaign that would communicate the truths just discovered.

After a study of God's grace, for instance, have your group come up with a way to advertise to the world what the Bible tells us are the benefits and advantages of God's grace to human beings. One group might be assigned to create billboards, another to create magazine ads, park bench ads or any of the multitude of ads that are normally displayed.

Because advertisements are usually large, colorful and eye-catching, make sure to have lots of large paper and colored felt pens on hand.

Magnetic Teaching

CD Covers

Music and music images are part of most teenagers' lives. After reading a passage of Scripture, ask your students to create a CD cover for a collection of songs dealing with the subject studied.

If your students have studied the Lord's Prayer, you could have each small group take one part of that prayer to make the title for their CD ("Holy Be Your Name," "Forgive Us Our Sins," and so on). They could then create artistic images to reflect that idea as well as song titles to go along with it.

To make it really cool, get your hands on some CD cases and have your students create their art to fit into the actual case.

Self-Adhesive Teaching

Do-It-Yourself Booklets

With paper, black pens, a stapler, cutting board and a copy machine, your group can create cool little booklets that tell of God's wisdom.

One 8 1/2 by 11 inch sheet can be folded, cut and stapled to form a small 12-page booklet. The most difficult part of making these booklets is getting the order of the pages right so that the book reads properly when assembled. Use the illustration on page 62 as your layout model for students to follow.

Explore your Bible lesson and have your students retell the story or create a modern version that can be told and summarized in 12 pages. Once you double-check the final layout, copy front and back sides and then distribute the copies to the group for them to cut, staple and share with their friends.

If you have access to clip art and a computer for clear type, these booklets can look pretty impressive. If you have a source for making color copies, create the booklets in full color!

62

Self-Adhesive Teaching

Book Covers

Creating book covers is a great activity to do around the beginning of the school year. Cut sheets of butcher paper into squares. (The typical size for a book cover is 22" x 11".) Have enough for each student to make three or four covers.

Drag out colored marking pens and ask your students to design book covers that would both present their faith and also remind them to walk with God while in school. You can tie this activity in with a lesson about keeping our Christian example strong.

Magnetic Teaching

Self-Adhesive Drama, Video and Theater

You don't have to be a skilled actor to learn through drama, which can be used in many different ways. Most of the drama ideas suggested here take little or no preparation. They are spontaneous, lightly scripted and tons of fun.

The key for using drama is to make sure that everyone is involved. This may mean that some kids become rocks or swaying trees as part of the presentation.

Much of the effort and learning in using drama comes from assembling the script based on the Scripture text studied. The presentation is the frosting on the cake.

Self-Adhesive Teaching

Pantomime

Probably the easiest form of drama is a pantomime. It requires few if any props and can be done without dialog. Working in small groups enables a pantomime to be created and performed with active participation from everyone.

Any number of biblical situations can be acted out, as can a vast number of everyday life responses to God's truths. For instance, using James' teaching about favoritism (see James 2:1-4), a great two-part drama could be staged showing how people were being excluded in the meetings of the early church and how a person might be left out in a typical youth group meeting today.

Magnetic Teaching

Paper-Bag Puppet Show

An entirely different kind of drama can be created using puppets made of simple materials such as paper lunch bags, yarn, cotton, fabric scraps, glue and felt-tip pens. While a bit juvenile for high school students, even their interest and energy will get fired up for this kind of production if they are given an opportunity to perform for younger kids.

Have your students read a passage, develop a script, make a backdrop and create puppet characters. Sound effects, lighting and narration can also be added.

Try some of the parables of Christ for great material. Dramatic situations such as Jesus' encounter with the demon-possessed man (see Luke 8:26-39) are also terrific.

Self-Adhesive Teaching

Interview and Talk Show

Try exploring the truths of the Bible by creating a radio or TV talk show that parodies today's popular shows. Interviews can be done live or by using tape recorders or video cameras.

Have your students explore a Scripture passage and then assign various individuals within the group different roles in the interview.

Using the story of David and Goliath (see 1 Samuel 17) as an example, interviews could be set up with all the principle characters: Saul, David, Goliath and the soldiers. You would need few costumes or props. Both the interviewer and "guests" could create and rehearse the list of questions in advance so that the interview comes off smoothly.

Magnetic Teaching

Bible Jeopardy

Steal the format from the well-known TV game show. Divide your students into teams, read assigned passages and then play a game of Bible Jeopardy. Make up categories such as "Biblical Names That Begin with 'J'," "Holy Land Bodies of Water," "Ancient History," "Angels," "Musical Instruments" or "Rhyme Time." Then write five questions that pertain to each category, progressing in degree of difficulty from the easiest to the hardest. Award the highest points for the hardest questions. You can also use this idea to explore application of biblical truths.

Self-Adhesive Teaching

Captain Clay Video Show

Using colored clay or play dough, paper backdrops, and odds and ends, your students can create a video show that humorously but accurately portrays ideas or events from the Bible.

Each group needs a large table to use as a stage. Assign each group a passage of Scripture upon which to build a script. A long passage can be divided among the groups to become a "series."

Students then fashion characters out of clay and shoot them on video from various angles using offstage narration, music and sound effects to round out the story. Make sure to acquire enough video cameras so that groups don't have to wait on each other to start filming.

For example, the story of Jonah could show a clay model Jonah at home, on board ship, in the fish and at Nineveh. Or groups using Jonah's story as a base could create contemporary examples of how people try to run from God.

Show the completed stories to the group and watch them howl in learning laughter!

Magnetic Teaching

19

Freeze Frame

This is a very simple but fun way for teens to demonstrate the application of the Bible's truths in everyday life.

Assign your groups the passage of Scripture you've chosen. Each group is to create living "photos," one for each truth or incident from the passage. With the help of a narrator, the group scrambles into position and freezes in that position for a few moments before moving to the next "photo."

The results are a riot to watch and fun to be involved in. If you like, take pictures of the living photos.

Self-Adhesive Teaching

Ask the Expert

Invite an expert to visit your group and answer questions from students about his or her area of expertise. For example, if you want to study cults and other religions, you might find someone in your church who is an ex-Mormon or Jehovah's Witness. These folks have insights into the beliefs of particular cults that students don't often hear.

Before the visit, have your kids write out questions on 3" x 5" cards. They will learn a lot from this kind of interview since they are involved by asking the questions.

Magnetic Teaching

21

Do It!

Rather than merely studying about a Christian virtue, plan for your group to go out and do it. Right there, right on the spot.

For example, perhaps you are exploring the Scripture that tells us to "be doers of the word" (James 1:22). Put your group into immediate action by grabbing buckets, rags, soap and going out to the church parking lot to look for the dirtiest car and give it a bath (unknown to the owner). Yes, in church clothes and all!

Your teens will be excited by both the suddenness and the stealth of being an instant doer of the Word.

Self-Adhesive Teaching

Biblical Post-it® Notes

Everyone is familiar with Post-it® notes. Bring a pile of them to your group meeting and use them to help illustrate the lesson you are teaching. For example, ask your students to explore passages of Scripture, write the key words they find on Post-it® notes and then hang them around their work space. Everyone will be able to see what others have come up with. Or, ask kids to imagine what kind of things various biblical characters might have put on Post-it® notes had they been around then. The story of David and Bathsheba via Post-it® notes is one that won't be easily forgotten.

Section 4

Sticky Moments

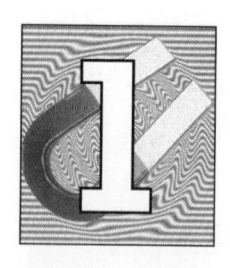

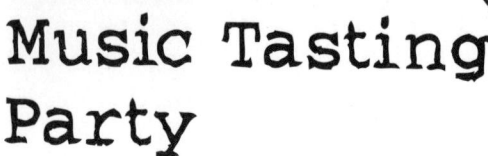

Music Tasting Party

Theme: Encourage pure and good thoughts with pure and good music.
Scripture: Philippians 4:8
Materials: A number of CD players and headsets; music posters; Christian music videos; video projector or TV; a ton of Christian CDs; refreshments

The Christian community often gripes about the terrible nature of youth-oriented music. The music tasting party will expose your students to a wide variety of Christian artists who provide a better music alternative.

Most Christian music is sold in Christian bookstores. Because few teens patronize these stores, they are often unaware of the wonderful variety of great Christian music available for those who would rather fill their minds with good stuff. The music tasting party is a great way to have fun and inform your students about the godly options available in the music scene.

To make this a fun event, you will want to create a club environment with the right lighting, food and drink, music videos projected on the wall, lots of music posters and so forth. You may want to go all out and hire a band to end the evening. You could even require a cover charge at the door.

Set up a few tables with CD players, headsets and CDs. Place the CD jewel cases next to the players so teens can see who is playing and check out their lyric sheets. Before the party, mooch as many CD players as you need so that most or all of your partygoers can be tasting music at the same time.

Get your hands on as many CDs from current Christian artists as possible. Asking musically oriented kids in your youth group is one way to do this. Another great way is to invest a few hundred bucks and pick up dozens of new releases from the Christian music ministry Interl'inc. They send out music and videos on a quarterly basis, but you can get a whole year's worth just by asking. These folks will set you up with gobs of CDs, posters and even lesson plan outlines for many of the songs. Contact them at 1-800-725-3300. Explain to them that you are doing a music tasting party and would like to get a year's worth of music at one time. They will be glad to help. (If money is a problem for your church, sell or auction the CDs at the party. If you plan to do this, tell everyone to bring extra bucks.)

The end result of the evening will probably do more to help your kids stick good things into their heads and hearts than all the negative preaching could ever accomplish.

Magnetic Teaching

Taking God's Name in Vain

Theme: Treat God's name with respect.
Scripture: Exodus 20:7

For this idea you need a good-natured kid to "pick on" during class time. Let's say you've decided to choose a student named John. In the process of your lesson on the subject, call out John's name. When he responds, make no reply; simply ignore him. Continue to do this during the course of your lesson. This could make John really irritated, which is exactly the point. In fact, you may make everyone irritated at you.

For more impact, use John's name in vain in the same manner that people use God's: "Oh my John!" or worse. String these kinds of expletives into your talk and you will be sure to get the troop's attention.

After you have abused the name of your student, turn your study into a discussion. Point out that one way we take God's name in vain is to call upon him without desiring to speak to him. Ask your students questions such as:

- **How do you think John felt to have his name called but to have no response when he answered? Do you think God feels the same way when we ignore him?**
- **John, how did it make you feel to hear your name used as an expletive? What does this teach us about using God's name this way?**
- **Is there something unique or special about a person's name that makes him or her protective of it? What would that be? What about God's name?**
- **What does taking God's name in vain tell you about those who do it?**

Sticky Moments

Instant Prayer Reminders

Theme: Pray for each other.
Scriptures: Psalm 105:3; Philippians 4:6; Colossians 4:2
Materials: Computer; printer; package of business cards that can run on the printer

Ask your students to write down something that they would like others to pray about for them. Collect all the prayer requests and print them out on business cards, a set for each student. Invite your teens to select one of the cards each day and to pray for the person and the specific needs listed.

Not only will this exercise remind your students to pray for each other, but it is a great way to build in them the discipline of prayer.

77

Magnetic Teaching

4

Filled or Flat?

Theme: Be filled with the Holy Spirit.
Scriptures: Romans 8:11; 1 Corinthians 3:16
Materials: One large balloon; marking pen

Here is a simple tool to help your students remember the idea that allowing Christ to fill their lives will make them much more effective than they could ever be on their own.

Ahead of time, use a marking pen to write a word (such as love) or draw a picture or symbol on an inflated balloon. Let the air out.

Discuss a life without the Holy Spirit breathing into it. Point out that it is very similar to the balloon—people can have love, but their capacity is diminished. Their lives are flat in contrast to what they could be.

Begin to inflate the balloon and point out the obvious growth, dimension and greatness of the things God wants to do in us. Our potential for godliness is limited only by how much we allow the Holy Spirit to fill us.

Sticky Moments

Jerk Day

Theme: Love the unlovely.
Scripture: Matthew 5:43-48
Materials: Wanted posters from the post office; newspaper and magazine clippings of various crimes, criminals, scoundrels and thugs

Jesus said to love those who are our enemies. We are to love the scum, the undesirable. But what does this look like and how can it be played out in real life? Saturate your students with the worst that modern society has to offer. Look at some wanted posters. Discuss heinous crimes and those who commit them. Tell about personal incidents of being ripped off or cheated. It shouldn't take too long to have your kids in the lynch mob mood.

Throw them a curve by jumping into a study of Christ's teachings about loving those who are anything but nice guys. Discuss what it means to show love to bad people. Ask questions such as these:

- **Could you obey Christ's command and still find a criminal guilty if you were on the jury?**
- **Does love mean letting someone off the hook for their deeds or being gullible?**

Take time to pray for those people whose crimes and sins you've talked about.

79

Magnetic Teaching

You Just Never Know

Theme: Always live in spiritual readiness.
Scripture: Matthew 24:36-51
Materials: A windup alarm clock; heavy-duty tape

Before your students arrive, tape the alarm clock securely to the bottom of a chair that you are certain a student will sit in. Try to set your alarm to go off at the strategic point in your lesson. During your teaching time, make sure to strongly emphasize that we never know when Christ might return or when we might go to meet him.

Point out that not one of us has any guarantee on our lives. The time might run out at any point. We should not be unprepared. You can build on this idea: **"Our lives are ticking away second by second towards our eternal destination. Some will be called to exit suddenly and without warning. When God says our time is up, our time is up."**

Somewhere in this process the alarm will sound, startling the student in the chair and those around him. Use this alarming moment as an example of what you have been describing in the lesson about the uncertainty of life.

Sticky Moments

7 Do Not Open

Theme: Our sin nature compels us to break God's laws.
Scripture: Genesis 3
Materials: A box with an easy-to-open lid and a sign on it saying "Do Not Open"

Place your box on a table in the youth meeting room. Be far away from it or out of the room as students arrive. If you have a group of junior highers, it's a sure bet that someone is going to see that box and peek in it. Others will struggle not to peek. High school students may have more self-control, but they will want to take a look as well.

A booby trap in the box would add to the fun, if you can create one. Try hooking up a loud doorbell, the ringer type, with hidden wires. An assistant could secretly fire it off when the box is opened. This way you would know without question that someone had disobeyed the sign!

Before you start teaching, ask if anyone wanted to open the box but resisted the urge. Spring into your lesson on sinful human nature or temptation. Everyone will understand that it pertains to them.

Magnetic Teaching

Appreciation Party

Theme: Show love and encouragement to others.
Scriptures: Philippians 2:1, 2; Hebrews 3:13; 10:24
Materials: Food; party decorations; invitations; a card

Every Christian knows that he or she should show appreciation to others. We just don't do it enough. An appreciation party will make a lesson on encouragement spring to life.

Challenge your students to help you create an appreciation party for someone in the church or youth group who deserves to be recognized but seldom is.

Keeping it a secret from that person if you can, organize groups to work on the various aspects of throwing a good party: invites, munchies, tributes, etc. Have one group create an appreciation card and make sure that everyone writes something in it as well as signs it.

Your group will be excited to be able to put into action the principles of gratitude they have discovered.

Sticky Moments

The Cost of Freedom

Theme: Freedom has a price tag.
Scripture: 1 Peter 2:13-17
Materials: As many bill stubs and receipts as you can gather in a month before this lesson

Most teens long for freedom from the constraints of their parents, schools and chores. Some feel it would be wonderful to launch into the world with absolute freedom and carefree living. The wiser among us realize that there is no such thing as total freedom. Even our freedom in Christ calls us to responsibilities and moral rules.

Get a good discussion going about freedom by asking your students questions such as these:
- **Are you looking forward to becoming 18? Why?**
- **What freedom do you miss now that you think you will have as an adult?**

After a bit of discussion, point out that freedom does come with a price tag. Dramatically dump a month's worth of bill stubs and receipts out in front of the students. Comment: **"This is what it costs me each month to have my freedom as an adult. And since it costs me, I am not really free to do as I please. I have restraints, obligations and commitments that come with my freedom."**

Quickly go over the approximate costs of your various budget categories: food, rent, utilities, vehicle, insurance, entertainment and the like. Point out that even as adults, life requires us to live responsibly and to

83

work hard.
　Slide into a lesson about freedom in Christ and how as Christians we must balance our spiritual freedom and privileges with hard work and right living.

Sticky Moments

Obituary Wake-Up Call

Theme: Contemplate death in order to live a life of meaning.
Scripture: Colossians 4:5
Materials: A week's worth of obituaries from your local newspaper, pasted together and copied; blank paper; writing utensils

There is nothing better to get a person focused on living life than seriously considering death. Obituaries are the final word on the nature and accomplishments of an individual. They are sobering reading.

Distribute obituaries for students to read. Discuss some of these things with your group:

- **What does this announcement tell you about the person who died?**
- **How meaningful or significant was this person's life?**
- **Do you think brief obituaries mean that the person didn't accomplish much?**
- **What would you want in your obituary?**
- **What do you think God would want to see in your obituary?**
- **How would you like to be remembered?**

Have students write their own imaginary obituaries based on what they have just learned.

Magnetic Teaching

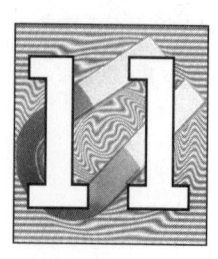

11

Honesty First

Theme: A Christian should be honest and trustworthy.
Scriptures: Deuteronomy 25:15, 16; Proverbs 12:22; Luke 6:31

How honest are the teens you work with? How they answer that question may be less than truthful!

Get a discussion about honesty going and force some real soul-searching by using our battery of very uncomfortable questions; you can add many more of your own:

- If you found a bag of cash with no name on it, what would you do?
- If you found a wallet with several hundred dollars and identification, what would you do?
- If someone unknowingly had a very valuable sports card in the dime bin of a garage sale, would you speak up?
- Would you tell the truth if someone who was unattractive but felt that you were a good friend asked you point-blank, "Do you think I'm pretty?"
- If you were asked by the teacher why you didn't turn in your homework, would you make up a story to save a grade?
- Would you drive better with a cop behind you?
- Would you exaggerate the truth to feel accepted in a group you admire?
- Would you lie to a friend's parents who asked if their kid had ditched school?
- If you were given too much change at a store, would you keep it?
- Would you tell someone if your friends were using drugs, driving while drunk or shoplifting?
- If you got free cable TV by accident, would you report it to the cable company?

- Would you tape-record a CD so a friend wouldn't have to buy the album?
- Would you litter if there was no one around to see you?

- If a friend planted a bug in her food in order to get the meal for free, would you squeal?

Magnetic Teaching

The Tapestry

Theme: God has a perfect plan for our lives, even if we don't see it.
Scriptures: Psalm 33:11; Isaiah 58:11; James 1:17; 2 Peter 3:9
Materials: A small tapestry rug or needlepoint design

This activity provides a very simple illustration of a profound spiritual concept. Many times we don't understand why God allows some events to happen. Things don't make sense and it is easy to get frustrated about the various unanswerable "whys" of life.

As you begin to assure your students that God indeed has a plan for them, pull out a tapestry rug or needlepoint design (without revealing the face of the design) and, holding the back for your students to see, ask them if they can figure out what the picture is.

Depending on the complexity of the design, your students may or may not be able to "get the picture." Flip the tapestry around and the picture is clear.

This is a perfect way to show how God, who stitches the events of our lives together with his perfect love, knows exactly what he is doing—even if we don't get it from our vantage point.

Sticky Moments

How Am I Doing?

Theme: Keep your word and commitments to God.
Scriptures: 1 Corinthians 4:2; Matthew 25:14-23
Materials: Envelopes; paper; stamps

Here is a great way to have your students remind themselves of a commitment they have made or an area in their lives they are working on.

After a motivating Bible study or event such as a retreat, ask your students to write a personal letter reminding themselves of the commitment they have made. Ask them to address an envelope and seal their letter in it. Tell them, **"You may not remember for too long the commitment you have made, but in a few months you will get a letter from yourself to help remind you of where you ought to be in your Christian walk."**

Collect the letters and drop them in the mail a few months later. Students often will snap to attention when they see the progress—or lack of it—they have made.

Magnetic Teaching

14

Bible, Be Gone

Theme: Store God's Word in your hearts.
Scriptures: Joshua 1:8; Psalm 37:31; 119:11
Materials: Paper; pencils

Help your students see the importance of committing the Bible to memory with this exercise. As they come into the room, confiscate all Bibles. Tell your students, **"I want you to imagine that you live in a country that has just outlawed owning a Bible. Your job is to create a Bible based on your memory that we can use when we get together. Recall and write down as many verses as you can remember . . . but put them down only if you know where they are found in the Bible."**

Give your group blank paper, pencils and a few minutes to go at it. They will no doubt be surprised at how few passages and their locations they can come up with.

Underscore this lesson by relating situations when Christians had no Bibles and were forced to rely on their memory of Scriptures, such as POWs or those persecuted for their faith. Urge your students to think of occasions when they have no Bible handy but need to recall Scripture—for example, times of temptation, witnessing to friends and challenges from teachers. Be prepared to provide students who are motivated to memorize with a basic list of essential verses.

Sticky Moments

The Challenge of the Week

Theme: Exercise spiritual discipline.
Scriptures: Romans 6:12-14; 1 Corinthians 9:24-27; 2 Timothy 2:1-7

Invite your students to take a new and sometimes difficult challenge each week. For example, challenge them to go for a week without watching TV. Then for another week challenge them to do what they are asked by a parent the very first time without comment. The challenges can go on and on: Challenge them to share their faith with someone that week, to go a week without candy or soda, to give away any money they make that week to charity.

Each week encourage your students to talk about the previous challenge, their successes and failures. This may not be for everyone, but for those who like a challenge, it can be both fun and exciting!

Section 5

The Magnetic Field

Sometimes a subject is better taught using all the senses. In these cases, drag your group away from the church building and out into places where the sticking power is greatest.

Naturally, you will have to line up your transportation in advance, and if you will be gone longer than the normal class time, make sure to let parents know.

Most of these ideas can be done right around your hometown. You can also improvise: for example, go stand around a smelly dumpster rather than make the drive to the city dump or buy a sack of manure and dump it on the church lawn if actual cow droppings are hard to find.

You can probably think of a lot of other places to go that would illustrate a biblical truth. Use the following road trips as imagination starters.

The Magnetic Field

Greenhouse

Theme: Grow as a Christian.
Scriptures: John 7:37, 38; 8:12; 15:1-17; Hebrews 10:25

A trip to a local greenhouse, especially in winter, is a great way to focus on the subject of Christian growth. Let your students explore the place, looking for things that serve as object lessons for the various elements of growth—food, water, warmth, protection and so forth. As they share their insights, be sure they explain how these things speak of ways Christians can grow spiritually. For example, Jesus is called living water and light, which means we can grow by soaking up and basking in his Word.

Ask questions such as these:
- **What does the Bible say about bearing fruit?**
- **What is the purpose of fruit from a tree?**
- **What is the purpose of Christian fruit?**
- **What might a weed represent in the Christian life?**
- **In what way is God like a farmer?**

93

Magnetic Teaching

2

City Dump

Theme: The things of this world fail; invest in eternity.
Scripture: Matthew 6:19-24

This lesson stinks! A trip to the local landfill contrasts the fate of all those material things we hold so dear with the eternal rewards of a life invested in Christ. Note: Be sure your group comes dressed appropriately in their grubbies. You may want to get permission from the owners of the dump beforehand to allow your group to participate in this on-site event.

This lesson works best if your students don't know where you are taking them. As you drive them to the dump, pass by the rich part of town or the expensive stores and car dealers. As the kids get an eyeful of what money can buy, ask questions that will probe their attitudes toward possessions and ambitions:

- **What kinds of things would you like to buy?**
- **Can money buy happiness?**
- **What do possessions tell about the possessor?**

At the dump, sit on or near the yucky stuff and read Matthew 6:19-24. Point out that the junk was once important to someone, but now means nothing and is less than worthless. Have teens suggest specific ways they could earn eternal rewards in Heaven. Responses could include telling others about Christ, befriending the friendless, getting to know God better and helping you around the church.

The Magnetic Field

Track and Field

Theme: Run the Christian race with purpose and perseverance.
Scriptures: 1 Corinthians 9:24-27; Hebrews 12:1-3

The Bible speaks of "running the race" (Hebrews 12:1). You can drive this important aspect of Christian life home by holding your study at the finish line of a track or the goal of a football or soccer field.

Start the lesson by challenging your students to race you in a short sprint. Ask them to describe the difference between successfully running a sprint and a marathon.

Dig into the suggested Scripture passages and ask questions like these:

- **What does the race represent?**
- **What prize do we compete for?**
- **How do we prepare ourselves to win this race?**
- **What are some things that hinder or tangle teenagers in this race?**

Have students decide individually on some sort of disciplined activity they can do this week to get themselves in shape to run the spiritual race. They might commit to reading a certain amount of Scripture each day, spending so many minutes in prayer or studying a certain book of the Bible with other Christians at school lunch.

Magnetic Teaching

The Cemetery

Theme: Consider carefully your eternal destination.
Scriptures: Psalm 103:14-16; Isaiah 5:8; Luke 20:34-38; 1 Thessalonians 4:13

Teaching at a graveside gives you a chance to get very serious about life and death. Before you begin, scout out the best location. The grave of a teenager or of a person known to many of your students heightens the impact. You can talk about the accomplishments of a known person's life or the people he touched in a godly way. The grave of an infant leads to discussions on why children die, why we allow abortion and why God allows suffering.

After you go through your Bible study, ask questions like these:

- **How would you live if you believed you ceased to exist at death?**
- **What do you think God wants us to do with our lives?**
- **Is it wrong for a believer to fear death?**
- **How can you know you are going to Heaven?**

Give students time to walk alone among the graves, thinking of their own mortality and God's call to live a set-apart life. Wrap up the meeting with a chance for students to write their own epitaph or eulogy.

The Magnetic Field

A Pigpen

Theme: Avoid life's pigpens: learn well the lessons of the prodigal son.
Scripture: Luke 15:11-32

Nothing beats a good old pig farm for a nauseating look at Christ's parable of the prodigal son. You might want to keep this one short!

As you drive to the pigpen, ask questions like these:
- **Have you ever run away from home? What happened?**
- **At what age is a person ready to leave home for good? Why?**
- **When you leave home, what new responsibilities will you have to take on immediately?**
- **In what ways should you expect your parents to "back you up" when you leave?**
- **What are some of the blessings of leaving home?**
- **What are some of the dangers of leaving home?**

After you go over the Scripture, while still at the pigpen, discuss the results of straying from God, using questions like these:
- **Jesus told this parable to a Jewish audience. What do you think they thought about a young man ending up with a bunch of "unclean" pigs?**
- **What might Jesus have used instead of a pigpen if he were teaching today in our society?**
- **What is the message of this parable? Who should listen to it?**
- **What should we do to ensure we don't end up in the pigpen of life?**

97

Magnetic Teaching

6

A Wheat Field

Theme: God will separate the believer from the unbeliever.
Scriptures: Matthew 3:11, 12; 13:24-30, 36-43

Fields of wheat figured mightily in Jesus' teachings. Referring to wheat, he touched on his death and resurrection (see John 12:23, 24), evangelism (Matthew 9:37, 38; John 4:35), bearing fruit (Matthew 13:3-8) and more. Jesus also used wheat and chaff to teach about the distinctions between genuine believers and the insincere.

If you can locate a wheat field nearby, and with the help and permission of the owner, allow your students to cut and winnow some wheat. As you go over the Scripture passages, discuss these questions:

- **What does the wheat signify in the passages?**
- **What do the chaff and weeds signify?**
- **What happens to the weeds and chaff?**
- **What happens to the wheat?**
- **Who separates the weeds from the wheat?**

The weeds and chaff symbolize sin and insincerity. Have students suggest the kinds of weeds and chaff they have to deal with in their Christian "wheat field."

98

The Magnetic Field

A Pile of Manure

Theme: Lose everything except Jesus and you have everything you need.
Scripture: Philippians 3:4-9

To Paul, gaining Christ made all the other accomplishments of his life look like rubbish—or, in the original Greek, "dung." Paul's sense of priority can be gained by your students in an unforgettable lesson held at the local dairy or cattle feed lot.

As you head out to the manure pile, involve your teens in a discussion of the merits, if any, of power, fame, status and wealth. Here are some sample questions:

- **If you could magically have anything you wanted, what would it be? Why?**
- **Is there anything particularly special about the celebrities people admire—movie stars, TV personalities, leaders of state, rock stars? If so, what? If not, why do you think people are so easily drawn to them?**
- **Who is justified in bragging because of his credentials?**
- **Can you think of any people in the Bible who could brag because of their accomplishments?**

Go over Philippians 3:4-9 with your students. Explain what the word "rubbish" meant to Paul and his attitude toward all the things he worked so hard to accomplish in light of his having now met and gained Christ. As you pull up to the manure, your students will sense—in more ways than one—just what Paul was saying.

On your way back to home base, help your students consider their own spiritual priorities by asking questions such as these:

- **Why is knowing and gaining Christ such a wonderful thing?**
- **Are Christians supposed to ignore accomplishments such as a good education and an important career? If not, what should be our**

Magnetic Teaching

attitude toward these things in light of today's lesson?
- What are some of the things that can sidetrack us from a love for Christ?
- How can we avoid these things?
- What do you suppose are the achievements that please God?

The Magnetic Field

Polluted Water

Theme: Keep yourself pure.
Scriptures: Matthew 5:8; Philippians 4:8; 1 Timothy 4:12; 5:22

Sin pollutes the Christian. Set up your Bible study next to a polluted stream or pond—unhappily, they aren't hard to find. Bring cleanup gear, including garbage bags and work gloves, for each person.

At the site, scoop up some scummy water with a glass. Offer to let anyone have a long, cool drink.

Go over the Scripture passages and ask these questions:

- **What is the definition of purity?**
- **What is spiritual purity?**
- **What are some specific things that make us spiritually impure?**
- **Which of these things are avoidable and which cannot be helped?**
- **Are most people concerned more about impurities they put into their bodies than the impurities they put into their minds?**
- **Do spiritually impure people have an effect on other people? If so, in what ways?**
- **What concerns should our youth group and church have about spiritually impure members?**

Discuss ways to filter out spiritual impurities:

- **What are some practical ways to deal with our mental impurities?**
- **Should a Christian stop listening to secular music and watching TV? If not, is there a line the Christian shouldn't cross? Where do we draw the line?**
- **What guidelines would you give new Christians to help them avoid spiritual pollution?**

After this lesson, clean up the site.

101

Magnetic Teaching

9

A Bakery

Theme: Be what you are: avoid hypocrisy.
Scripture: Luke 12:1, 2

Jesus really stuck it to the Pharisees regarding their hypocrisy, pride and phoniness. He likened their hypocrisy to yeast. But most teens today have no idea what yeast is, much less the meaning of Christ's words about the yeast or leaven of the Pharisees.

You can cause their knowledge to "rise" by showing them around a bakery. A donut shop is nice, especially if you pass around some samples.

Ask students to define leaven or yeast. If they cannot, explain that yeast is a fungus used in baking. As the yeast feeds on the sugars in the bread or donut dough, it emits gaseous by-products which cause the dough to rise.

Study the passage together and ask questions such as these:
- **What is hypocrisy?**
- **Why do you suppose Jesus used yeast to teach about hypocrisy?**
- **What are some areas of hypocrisy that Christians your age need to look out for?**
- **What damage can hypocrisy do to an individual? To our youth group?**
- **What are some practical ways to avoid or clean out the yeast of hypocrisy?**

Topical Index

Beauty	20
Bible's trustworthiness	46
Christian music	74
Confession	40
Death and eternity	35, 85, 96
Effects of sin	39
Encouragement	82
Fellowship with God	18
Foolishness	45
Forgiveness	39, 42
Freedom	83
Friendliness	41
God's design	29, 88
God's judgment	98
God's name	76
God's will	37
Greed	21, 22
Holy Spirit	78
Honesty	17, 86
Hypocrisy	102
Jesus' return	80
Keeping commitments	89
Labels	34
Loving the unlovely	79

Materialism 24, 26, 94
Memorizing the Word 90
Optimism 15
Prayer 77
Priorities 99
Purity 43, 101
Revenge 16
Running from God 97
Sacrificing for others 32
Spiritual discipline 91, 95
Spiritual growth 93
Talents 19
Temptation 81
Thankfulness 36
Urgency 28

Scripture Index

Genesis 3	81
Exodus 20:7	76
Deuteronomy 25:15, 16	86
Joshua 1:8	90
1 Samuel 17	67
Psalm 14:1	45
Psalm 33:11	88
Psalm 37:31	90
Psalm 40:5	37
Psalm 103:12	42
Psalm 103:14-16	96
Psalm 105:3	77
Psalm 119:11	90
Proverbs 1:7	45
Proverbs 11:22	20
Proverbs 12:18, 19	34
Proverbs 12:22	86
Proverbs 19:21	29, 37
Proverbs 20:22	16
Proverbs 24:26	17
Proverbs 31:30	20
Isaiah 1:18	39
Isaiah 5:8	96
Isaiah 43:25	42

Isaiah 55:1, 2 26
Isaiah 58:11 88
Jeremiah 29:11-13 37
Joel 2:12, 13 39
Matthew 3:1-17 57
Matthew 3:11, 12 98
Matthew 5:8 101
Matthew 5:38-42 16
Matthew 5:43-48 79
Matthew 6:19-24 94
Matthew 6:24 . . . . .26, 46
Matthew 7:21 37
Matthew 7:26 45
Matthew 9:37, 38 98
Matthew 11:1-19 57
Matthew 12:34-37 34
Matthew 13:3-8 98
Matthew 13:24-30, 36-43 98
Matthew 13:44 24
Matthew 14:1-12 57
Matthew 18:21, 22 46
Matthew 24:36-51 80
Matthew 25:14-23 89
Matthew 25:14-29 19
Matthew 25:35-40 32
Matthew 28:16-20 28
Mark 3:35 37

Scripture Index

Mark 9:41	32
Luke 3:11	32
Luke 6:31	86
Luke 8:26-39	66
Luke 12:1, 2	102
Luke 12:13-21	21, 56
Luke 15:11-32	97
Luke 20:34-38	96
John 4:35	98
John 7:37, 38	93
John 8:12	93
John 12:23, 24	98
John 14:15	46
John 14:16, 17	37
John 15:1-17	93
Acts 2	51
Acts 11:29	32
Romans 3:10-18	39
Romans 4:8	39
Romans 6:12-14	91
Romans 7:21-25	39
Romans 8:1	50
Romans 8:6	22
Romans 8:11	78
Romans 8:28	19, 29
Romans 12:2	37
Romans 12:17	16

1 Corinthians 3:12, 13 24
1 Corinthians 3:16, 17 . . . . .43, 78
1 Corinthians 4:2 89
1 Corinthians 9:24-27 . . . . .91, 95
1 Corinthians 15:52-57 35
2 Corinthians 4:17, 18 15
2 Corinthians 5:20, 21 18
Galatians 6:7 22
Philippians 2:1, 2 82
Philippians 3:4-9 99
Philippians 4:6 77
Philippians 4:8 . . . . .74, 101
Colossians 1:11, 12 36
Colossians 3:9, 10 17
Colossians 4:2 77
Colossians 4:5 85
1 Thessalonians 1:6 15
1 Thessalonians 4:13 96
1 Thessalonians 5:15 16
1 Thessalonians 5:16 15
1 Thessalonians 5:18 36
2 Thessalonians 1:6 16
1 Timothy 4:12 101
1 Timothy 5:22 101
1 Timothy 6:9, 10 . . . . .21, 26
2 Timothy 2:1-7 91
Titus 1:8 41

Scripture Index

Titus 2:7 17
Hebrews 3:1 43
Hebrews 3:13 . . . . .36, 82
Hebrews 8:12 42
Hebrews 10:24 82
Hebrews 10:25 93
Hebrews 12:1-3 95
James 1:17 88
James 1:22 72
James 2:1-4 . . . . .41, 65
James 3:5-10 34
James 4:8 18
1 Peter 2:13-17 83
1 Peter 3:3, 4 20
1 Peter 4:9 41
2 Peter 3:9 88
1 John 1:9 40